MARGARET McALLISTER is an award-winning author who comes from the north-east of England. Before writing full-time she taught drama and dance, cleaned churches and worked in a retreat house. She lives in Northumberland with her husband Tony and has three grown-up children. She is also the author of *15 Things Not to Do with a Baby*, published by Frances Lincoln.

HOLLY STERLING was born in Dublin and grew up in southern England. She studied Illustration and Design at the University of Sunderland, graduating with first class Honours. In 2013 she gained a Master of Fine Art with Distinction from Edinburgh College of Art, and in the same year she was Highly Commended for the Macmillan Illustration Prize and was a winner of the Seven Stories/Frances Lincoln Illustration Competition. Holly also competes for her country in karate; she is a double National Champion and Gold, Silver and Bronze medallist at World and European Championships. She lives in Sunderland. She has also illustrated *15 Things Not to Do with a Baby,* and written and illustrated *Hiccups!* both published by Frances Lincoln.

Don't miss the first hilarious title!

To Joseph, my first grandchild — M.M.

For Mum, Nanny, Grandma, Trish and Grannies everywhere. — H.S.

First published in Great Britain and in the USA in 2016 by Frances Lincoln Children's Books.
This paperback edition first published in Great Britain in 2017 by Frances Lincoln Children's Books,
74-77 White Lion Street, London N1 9PF
QuartoKnows.com
Visit our blogs at QuartoKnows.com

A CIP catalogue record for this book is available from the British Library.

ISBN 978-1-84780-913-1

Illustrated with watercolour, pencil and 'printed' textures.

Printed in China

1 3 5 7 9 8 6 4 2

15 things NOT to do with a Granny

Margaret McAllister

Illustrated by Holly Sterling

Frances Lincoln
Children's Books

A **granny** is a wonderful person to have in your life. If you're really lucky, you might have two grannies.

Follow these simple rules
to make sure every granny
is a happy granny.

Don't...

hide an **elephant** in your granny's bed.

Don't...

give her **squashed jelly beans** on toast for breakfast,

or put leftover
spaghetti
in her handbag.

Don't...

wear her **pants** on your head,

or use her **make-up** on your teddy bear.

Don't...

race her on a **skateboard**.

(She might win.)

Don't...

To Granny

give her a **crocodile** for her birthday,

or interrupt her doing **karate**.

Don't...

bang a **drum** to wake her up.

In fact, don't make any **loud noises**
when she's resting.

Don't... ask her to read too many **books** at once,

or forget to **share** her.

Don't...

send her up to the **moon** in a rocket.

Never...

swap her for a giraffe,

or **someone** else's granny.

DO...

go for walks,

listen to her,

play,

...love her. Lots.
She loves you!

Also illustrated by Holly Sterling for
FRANCES LINCOLN CHILDREN'S BOOKS

HICCUPS!
Holly Sterling

How do you stop the hiccups?

Find out what happens when Ruby's puppy Oscar gets the hiccups.
Ruby tries all kinds of things, from hoppity-hop and slurpity-slurp
to her special magic spell. But nothing seems to work… !

ISBN: 978-1-84780-674-1

Frances Lincoln titles are available from all good bookshops.
You can also buy books and find out more about your favourite titles,
authors and illustrators on our website: www.franceslincoln.com